COMETS AND METEORS

SOLAR SYSTEM

Lynda Sorensen

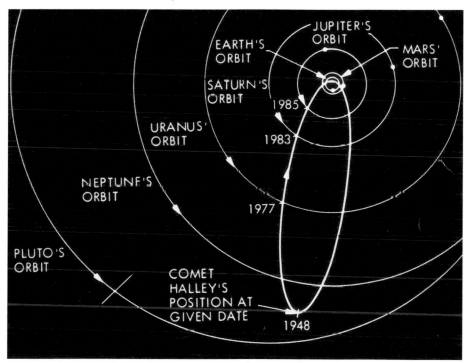

The Rourke Corporation, Inc.
Vero Beach, Florida 32964

Edited by Sandra A. Robinson

PHOTO CREDITS
All photos courtesy NASA except page 17 © Breck Kent; cover
and page 21 paintings for NASA by Donald E. Davis

Library of Congress Cataloging-in-Publication Data

Sorensen, Lynda, 1953-
     Comets and meteors / by Lynda Sorensen.
          p.   cm. — (The Solar system)
     Includes index.
     Summary: Describes the nature and movements of comets and
meteors and examines what happens to meteors after they hit the
Earth.
     ISBN 0-86593-277-8
     1. Comets—Juvenile literature. 2. Meteors—Juvenile literature.
3. Meteorites—Juvenile literature. [1. Comets. 2. Meteors.
3. Meteorites.] I. Title. II. Series: Solar system (Vero Beach, Fla.)
QB721.5.S67   1993
523.6—dc20   93-16690
                                                                    CIP
                                                                    AC

TABLE OF CONTENTS

COMETS

Comets are frozen masses of ice, rocks, gases and dust—old snowballs rocketing through space. Like the Earth, a comet travels around the sun in a path called an **orbit.** A comet's orbit is long and narrow.

When a comet's path nears the sun, some of the ice changes from a solid to a gas. At night, the sun's light makes the gas glow like a fuzzy ball of light.

Comet Kohoutek, photographed in 1974 through the Schmidt telescope at the Catalina Observatory of the University of Arizona

PARTS OF A COMET

The solid, frozen center of a comet is its **nucleus** of rock and ice. A hazy cloud of gases called the **coma** surrounds the nucleus. The nucleus and coma together make the head of the comet. The head of a large comet may be 1 million miles across.

The comet's head has a long tail. The tail is a mix of gases and tiny solid pieces of the comet's head—set free by wind and the sun's heat.

A Lowell Observatory photo of Comet Halley after computer processing and the addition of false color

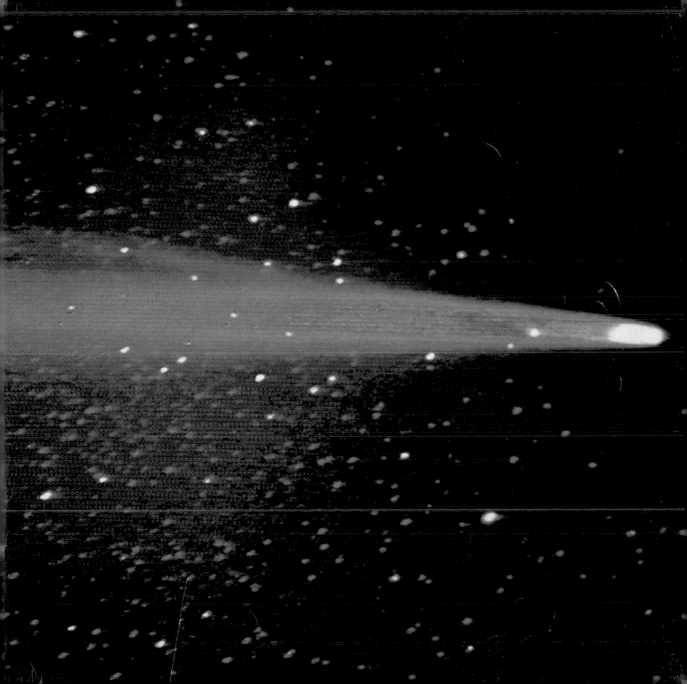

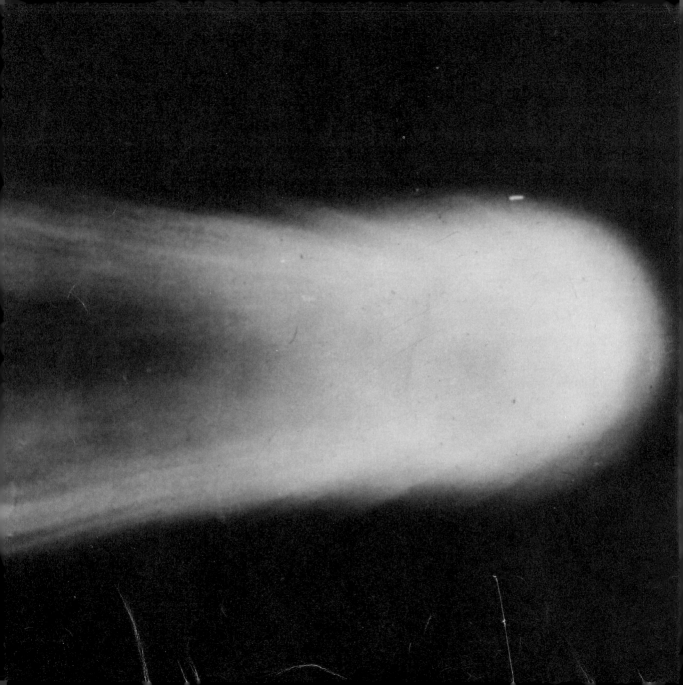

COMET HALLEY

Comet Halley is the brightest and best-known comet. It was named for Edmund Halley, a British scientist. Halley calculated in 1705 that this comet would pass the Earth every 76 years or so. Halley was correct.

Comet Halley is unusual because it is bright enough to be seen without a telescope. The tail of Comet Halley stretches 94 million miles. That is longer than the distance between the Earth and sun!

Last seen in 1986, Comet Halley should return in 2061.

Comet Halley was named for the British scientist who first predicted the return of a comet

DEATH OF A COMET

A comet's life is short compared to most space objects. Each time a comet passes by the sun, the sun's strong pulling force, called **gravity,** removes some of its gases and dust. A comet gradually grows dimmer and dimmer. Finally, the comet's gases are gone and it dies.

Comets with long orbits, however, may pass by the sun only once each 1,000 years. These comets last longer than comets with shorter orbits.

With each pass by the sun, a comet weakens

NASA's ICE spacecraft was equipped for the study of comets and other space bodies

NASA's Infrared Telescope Facility atop Mauna Kea, Hawaii, studies objects deep in space

METEOROIDS, METEORS AND METEORITES

Meteoroids are rocky objects in space that travel in orbits around the sun. They are smaller than planets. A meteoroid that leaves its orbit and plunges toward Earth is a **meteor.**

A falling meteor becomes fiery hot when it rubs against the Earth's air, or **atmosphere.** Meteors show up as streaking lights in the night.

Most meteors are very small. They burn up about 40 miles above Earth. A few large meteors survive their fall. The rock and metal chunks that fall to Earth are called **meteorites.**

This meteorite, found in Antarctica, may be from the planet Mars

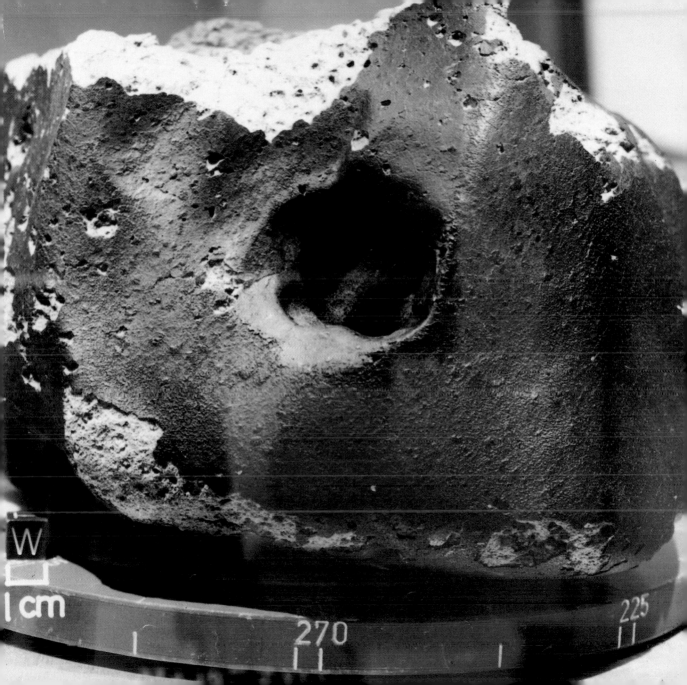

FAMOUS METEORITES

Meteorites may be the size of a pebble or huge boulders. The largest known meteorite is in Namibia, southwest Africa. This rock from outer space is 10 feet across and 3 feet thick. It weighs 60 tons.

A giant meteorite created Meteor Crater in Arizona about 50,000 years ago. Meteor Crater is nearly a mile wide and almost two football fields deep. The meteorite itself exploded into small pieces.

An airplane view of Meteor Crater, Arizona

METEOR SHOWERS

The Earth, moving through space, sometimes passes close to a comet's tail or to large groups of meteoroids—"space junk." At times, large amounts of this "junk" may fall to Earth.

Plunging at great speed, these meteors glow brightly until they burn up. From Earth, the show in the sky looks like a shower of brilliant streaks of light—a meteor shower.

A 19th century artist drew this image of the great meteor shower of November 12, 1833

DINOSAURS AND METEORITES

No one knows why dinosaurs disappeared from the Earth. One **theory,** or belief, to explain their disappearance involves a meteorite.

This theory says that a huge meteorite smashed into the Earth millions of years ago. (See the cover of this book.) The force of the giant meteorite's crash with Earth created a tremendous cloud of dust.

The dust was thick enough to block sunlight, according to the theory. Without light and warmth from the sun, plants and animals died. When the dust finally settled, the dinosaurs were gone forever.

This painting by Donald E. Davis—of a giant meteorite plunging into shallow seas off Mexico—shows the event that may have wiped out dinosaurs millions of years ago

STUDYING COMETS AND METEORS

Scientists who study comets, meteors and other heavenly bodies are called **astronomers.** Astronomers often work in buildings called **observatories.**

Observatories have special, high-powered telescopes. Astronomers use them to view and photograph distant objects in space.

The National Aeronautics and Space Administration (NASA) sends spacecraft into orbit to study and photograph space bodies such as Comet Halley.

Glossary

astronomer (uh STRON uh mer) — a scientist who studies the sun, moon, stars and other heavenly bodies

atmosphere (AT mus fear) — the air mass surrounding Earth

coma (KO ma) — the cloud of gases surrounding the nucleus of a comet; the head of a comet

gravity (GRAHV ih tee) — a powerful, invisible natural force that holds things in place

meteor (MEET ee er) — flaming piece of rock from space

meteorite (MEET ee er ite) — a meteor that reaches the Earth's surface without having burned up

nucleus (NU klee us) — the central, frozen part of a comet's head

observatory (uhb ZERV uh tor ee) — a placc where astronomers view and study the stars and solar system

orbit (OR bit) — the path that an object follows as it repeatedly travels around another object in space

theory (THEER ee) — a belief based on certain ideas and facts

INDEX